AF425972

Beyond Traditional Marriage: Navigating Live-in Relationships

C. P. Kumar
Reiki Healer
Roorkee - 247667, India

Copyright © 2023 C. P. Kumar

All rights reserved.

No part of this book may be reproduced or transmitted in any form or by any means, electronic or mechanical, including photocopying, recording, or by any information storage and retrieval system, without permission in writing from the author.

Disclaimer

While every effort has been made to ensure the accuracy and completeness of the content in this book, the author cannot guarantee that the information contained herein is error-free, up-to-date, or suitable for every individual circumstance.

The author shall not be held liable or responsible for any errors or omissions in the content of the book, nor for any damages, or losses that may arise from any actions taken based upon the suggestions or contents presented in the book.

Readers are advised to use their own judgment and discretion in applying the information provided in this book, and to consult with qualified professionals before taking any action based on the contents of this book. The author disclaims any and all liability or responsibility for any actions taken or not taken based on the information contained in this book.

CONTENTS

PREFACE

"Beyond Traditional Marriage: Navigating Live-in Relationships" is a comprehensive guide that explores the intricacies of modern partnerships. In today's evolving society, live-in relationships offer an alternative to traditional marriage and dating. This book delves into the definition and differentiation of live-in relationships, their advantages such as flexibility and freedom, as well as the challenges they present, including the lack of legal protection and rights.

Trust, commitment, and intimacy are explored as essential pillars within live-in relationships. The book addresses practical aspects such as sharing expenses and financial responsibilities, as well as the legal landscape surrounding cohabitation.

Parental acceptance, raising children, cultural variations, and acceptance are important considerations for those in live-in relationships. The book provides guidance on navigating these complex dynamics and milestones, as well as effective communication strategies.

Sexual compatibility, cohabitation agreements, psychological implications, and building a support system outside of marriage are also explored. Readers will gain insights into emerging patterns in live-in relationships and encounter reflections on the journey of navigating this unconventional path.

"Beyond Traditional Marriage: Navigating Live-in Relationships" serves as a valuable resource for individuals considering, currently in, or curious about live-in partnerships. It offers practical tools, knowledge, and real-life experiences to help forge successful and fulfilling relationships outside the bounds of traditional marriage.

C. P. Kumar
Reiki Healer
Former Scientist 'G', National Institute of Hydrology
Roorkee - 247667, India
E-mail: cpkumar@yahoo.com
Web: https://www.angelfire.com/nh/cpkumar/virgo.html

Introduction

In recent years, there has been a significant shift in societal norms and attitudes towards relationships and marriage. One of the most notable changes has been the rise of live-in relationships as an alternative to traditional marriage. These relationships, characterized by couples cohabiting without being legally married, have gained popularity among individuals seeking a different approach to commitment and partnership. In this chapter, we will explore the concept of live-in relationships, their historical and cultural context, the evolution of societal attitudes towards them, and what constitutes a live-in relationship in today's society.

Brief History and Cultural Context

The idea of cohabitation outside of marriage is not a new phenomenon. Throughout history, different cultures have embraced forms of living together without the formal institution of marriage. In ancient Rome, for example, the concept of "concubinage" allowed individuals to live together in a committed relationship without the legal obligations of marriage. Similarly, some indigenous communities around the world have practiced long-term cohabitation arrangements based on mutual consent and commitment.

In more recent times, the cultural context surrounding live-in relationships has evolved. The sexual revolution of the 1960s and 1970s challenged traditional values and norms, paving the way for increased acceptance of cohabitation. As societal attitudes towards premarital sex and cohabitation shifted, the concept of live-in relationships began to gain traction in Western societies. This trend continued into the 21st century, as individuals increasingly sought alternative forms of commitment and partnership.

Evolution of Societal Attitudes towards Live-in Relationships

Societal attitudes towards live-in relationships have undergone a considerable transformation over the past few decades. What was once viewed as unconventional or morally unacceptable is now widely accepted by a significant portion of the population. This change in perspective can be attributed to several factors.

Firstly, the feminist movement and the fight for gender equality have played a crucial role in shaping societal attitudes towards relationships. As women gained more autonomy and independence, the traditional gender roles associated with marriage became less appealing to many. Live-in relationships offered an alternative that allowed individuals to maintain their freedom and pursue personal goals while still enjoying the benefits of a committed partnership.

Secondly, the increasing divorce rates and disillusionment with traditional marriages have led many people to question the institution itself. The rise in divorce rates has highlighted the potential shortcomings of marriage and prompted individuals to seek alternatives that better suit their needs and desires. Live-in relationships provide a level of flexibility and freedom that can alleviate some of the pressures and expectations associated with traditional marriage.

Understanding the Concept: What Constitutes a Live-in Relationship?

Defining a live-in relationship can be somewhat challenging, as it can vary depending on cultural, personal, and legal contexts. However, certain elements are commonly associated with live-in relationships.

1. Cohabitation: The fundamental aspect of a live-in relationship is the shared living arrangement. Couples in live-in relationships reside together under one roof, often in a long-term and committed manner. Cohabitation distinguishes live-in relationships from other forms of non-cohabitating partnerships.

2. Mutual Commitment: Although live-in relationships do not involve a legal marriage contract, they typically involve a significant level of commitment between the partners. This commitment can be expressed through shared financial responsibilities, joint decision-making, and emotional support. While the level of commitment may vary among different couples, it remains a crucial aspect of live-in relationships.

3. Lack of Legal Marriage: Unlike traditional marriages, live-in relationships lack the legal recognition and formalities associated with marriage. Partners in live-in relationships do not enter into a legally binding contract or obtain a marriage license. This aspect grants individuals in live-in relationships more flexibility and freedom in their arrangement.

4. Intimate and Romantic Partnership: Live-in relationships are characterized by a deep emotional bond and romantic connection between the partners. These relationships often

involve sexual intimacy and may encompass shared goals, dreams, and future plans.

Conclusion

Live-in relationships have emerged as a viable alternative to traditional marriage, offering individuals the opportunity to form committed partnerships while maintaining a level of personal autonomy. The historical and cultural context surrounding live-in relationships has contributed to the evolution of societal attitudes, making them more widely accepted. Understanding the concept of live-in relationships involves recognizing the elements of cohabitation, mutual commitment, lack of legal marriage, and intimate and romantic partnership. As individuals continue to seek diverse ways of navigating relationships, live-in arrangements provide a unique path for those who desire commitment and partnership without the traditional constraints of marriage.

Introduction

In recent years, the concept of live-in relationships has gained significant traction, challenging the traditional notions of dating and marriage. Live-in relationships offer a unique middle ground between casual dating and the commitment of marriage, allowing individuals to explore a deeper level of partnership while maintaining a degree of independence. In this chapter, we will delve into the distinctions that set live-in relationships apart from dating and marriage, examining their legal status, recognition, and the advantages they offer.

Legal Status and Recognition of Live-in Relationships

Live-in relationships, also known as cohabitation or domestic partnerships, refer to couples who choose to live together without being married. While the legal recognition of such relationships varies across jurisdictions, many countries now acknowledge the rights and responsibilities of individuals in live-in partnerships. Some jurisdictions grant legal protection to cohabiting couples, offering certain rights similar to those enjoyed by married couples, such as property rights, financial obligations, and custody rights.

Advantages of Live-in Relationships

1. Flexibility and Independence: Live-in relationships provide a level of flexibility that may not be present in marriage. Couples can enjoy the benefits of a committed

partnership while maintaining their personal space and independence. This arrangement allows individuals to pursue their individual goals, careers, and hobbies, without the perceived constraints that often come with marriage.

2. Emotional Intimacy and Connection: Live-in relationships provide a platform for couples to foster emotional intimacy and connection. By sharing a living space, partners have the opportunity to experience the daily routines and challenges of life together, deepening their understanding of one another. Living together can also create a strong foundation for building trust, communication, and shared decision-making.

3. Shared Responsibilities and Financial Considerations: Cohabiting couples often share financial responsibilities, including rent or mortgage payments, household expenses, and other financial obligations. This shared financial commitment can provide a sense of stability and partnership, allowing couples to plan for the future collaboratively.

4. Testing Compatibility: Live-in relationships offer a way for couples to test their compatibility before making a lifelong commitment through marriage. Living together can provide insights into each partner's habits, values, and compatibility in terms of lifestyle, household responsibilities, and long-term goals. This period of cohabitation can help individuals make informed decisions about whether or not to pursue marriage.

5. Learning Conflict Resolution: Sharing a living space inevitably brings moments of disagreement and conflict. However, these challenges can also serve as opportunities for personal growth and learning effective conflict resolution skills. Live-in relationships allow couples to

navigate conflicts in a supportive environment, learning to communicate, compromise, and find solutions that work for both partners.

6. Alternative to Marriage: Live-in relationships provide an alternative to traditional marriage for those who may not wish to enter into a legally binding union. This option can be particularly appealing for individuals who have reservations about the legal and societal expectations that often accompany marriage.

Conclusion

Live-in relationships offer a distinct and evolving approach to intimate partnerships, standing between the casual nature of dating and the formal commitment of marriage. While live-in relationships may not be suitable for everyone, they provide a range of advantages, including flexibility, emotional intimacy, shared responsibilities, compatibility testing, and opportunities for personal growth. As society continues to evolve, it is crucial to recognize and respect the diverse forms of relationships that individuals choose, and live-in relationships are an important part of this evolving landscape.

Introduction

In recent years, traditional notions of marriage have evolved, and live-in relationships have gained significant prominence as an alternative form of commitment. The concept of living together without the legal bonds of marriage offers a unique set of advantages and challenges. This chapter delves into the topic of flexibility and freedom in live-in relationships, exploring the emotional and financial benefits, the idea of testing before marriage, as well as the potential disadvantages and challenges that couples may encounter.

Emotional and Financial Benefits

One of the key advantages of a live-in relationship is the flexibility it provides in terms of emotional and personal growth. Unlike marriage, which often comes with certain societal expectations and obligations, live-in relationships allow individuals to explore their own identities and pursue personal goals without feeling restricted. The absence of legal ties enables partners to have greater autonomy over their own lives while simultaneously sharing a deep emotional bond.

Moreover, living together offers an opportunity for couples to truly understand each other on a deeper level. The day-to-day interactions and shared responsibilities create an intimate space for emotional connection and growth. This increased understanding and compatibility can foster stronger bonds, enhancing the overall quality of the relationship.

Financial benefits also come into play in live-in relationships. Sharing expenses can alleviate the financial burden that often accompanies independent living. By pooling resources, couples can achieve financial stability more easily, enabling them to pursue shared dreams and aspirations. Additionally, the flexibility to determine financial arrangements without the legal constraints of marriage can promote open discussions about money management, fostering a healthier approach to financial matters.

Test Before Marriage

One of the common reasons why individuals opt for a live-in relationship is the desire to test compatibility before making a lifelong commitment. Living together can provide a glimpse into what married life might entail, allowing partners to assess their compatibility, negotiate differences, and make informed decisions about their future together.

This testing phase can be particularly valuable in identifying potential areas of conflict or incompatibility that may have otherwise been overlooked. It offers an opportunity to learn how to navigate challenges, communicate effectively, and find common ground. By experiencing the realities of day-to-day life together, couples can gain insights into each other's habits, preferences, and expectations, enabling them to make more informed choices about whether to proceed with marriage.

Disadvantages and Challenges of Live-in Relationships

While live-in relationships offer numerous benefits, they are not without their share of challenges. One of the primary concerns revolves around societal perceptions and stigma. Despite the increasing acceptance of non-traditional relationship models, live-in couples may still face judgment or disapproval from certain individuals or communities. Navigating these external pressures can be emotionally taxing and may require couples to develop a strong sense of resilience and self-assurance.

Furthermore, the absence of legal protection in live-in relationships can give rise to potential complications. Unlike married couples who have clear legal rights and responsibilities, live-in partners may face uncertainty in matters such as property ownership, inheritance, and decision-making during medical emergencies. It is crucial for couples in live-in relationships to have open and honest discussions about these issues and consider legal safeguards, such as cohabitation agreements, to protect their interests and ensure clarity.

Another challenge that may arise in live-in relationships is the lack of formal commitment. While the freedom and flexibility can be liberating, some individuals may yearn for the security and permanence that marriage offers. The absence of a formal commitment can sometimes lead to doubts or insecurities about the future of the relationship. Addressing these concerns through honest communication and understanding each partner's expectations can help mitigate potential conflicts.

Conclusion

Flexibility and freedom are the cornerstones of live-in relationships, offering individuals the chance to explore their personal growth, test compatibility, and enjoy the emotional and financial benefits of shared living. While challenges exist, open communication, mutual understanding, and legal safeguards can help couples navigate these potential obstacles. Ultimately, the decision to embark on a live-in relationship requires careful consideration, as it is a unique path that offers its own set of advantages and challenges. By embracing flexibility and freedom, couples can forge fulfilling and authentic relationships beyond the confines of traditional marriage.

Introduction

Live-in relationships, once considered unconventional, are increasingly becoming a prevalent form of partnership in today's society. Couples are opting for this arrangement as an alternative to traditional marriage, seeking freedom, independence, and flexibility. However, despite the growing acceptance, live-in relationships often lack legal protection and rights, leaving couples vulnerable in various aspects of their lives. This chapter aims to explore the challenges faced by individuals in live-in relationships due to the absence of legal safeguards, highlighting the social stigma and familial disapproval, emotional complexities and uncertainties, and the psychological and emotional dynamics that arise in such relationships.

Social Stigma and Familial Disapproval

One significant hurdle faced by couples in live-in relationships is the social stigma attached to their choice. While societal attitudes have evolved over time, many still hold traditional beliefs that perceive live-in relationships as morally wrong or socially unacceptable. Consequently, couples may encounter judgment, discrimination, and exclusion from their communities and social circles. Moreover, families, particularly parents and relatives, may disapprove of their choice, leading to strained relationships and emotional distress.

The absence of legal recognition further exacerbates the challenges faced by live-in couples. Without the legal status of marriage, they may be denied various social benefits and privileges, such as healthcare coverage, joint tax benefits, inheritance rights, and the ability to make decisions on behalf of their partner in medical emergencies. This lack of legal protection often leaves individuals in vulnerable positions, with limited avenues for redress in case of disputes or unfair treatment.

Emotional Complexities and Uncertainties

Live-in relationships are not without their emotional complexities and uncertainties. Unlike marriage, which has a predefined structure and societal expectations, live-in arrangements offer more flexibility but also come with increased ambiguity. Couples in live-in relationships must navigate a unique set of challenges, including defining the boundaries of their partnership, managing expectations, and ensuring mutual respect and commitment.

Moreover, the absence of legal protection can intensify emotional uncertainties. In the absence of clear legal frameworks, couples may find it difficult to address issues such as financial responsibilities, property ownership, and child custody. These uncertainties can lead to conflicts and emotional strain, as couples lack the legal safeguards that married individuals have to guide and protect their interests.

Psychological and Emotional Dynamics in Live-in Relationships

Live-in relationships often bring about distinctive psychological and emotional dynamics that differ from those experienced in traditional marriages. Without the legal commitment of marriage, individuals may experience a heightened sense of insecurity and fear of abandonment.

The absence of legal protection can make it easier for one partner to walk away from the relationship, leading to feelings of vulnerability and uncertainty.

Additionally, societal expectations and the lack of legal recognition can impact the emotional well-being of individuals in live-in relationships. The constant questioning and disapproval from others can erode self-esteem and create a sense of isolation. Moreover, without the legal rights associated with marriage, individuals may feel a sense of powerlessness or inequality within their partnership, which can strain the emotional bond between the couple.

Conclusion

While live-in relationships offer a non-traditional form of partnership for individuals seeking freedom and independence, the lack of legal protection and rights poses significant challenges. Social stigma and familial disapproval continue to create barriers, hindering the acceptance and recognition of live-in relationships in society. The emotional complexities and uncertainties faced by couples further highlight the need for legal safeguards to address issues of financial responsibility, property rights, and child custody. Additionally, the psychological and emotional dynamics in live-in relationships call for a deeper understanding and support to ensure the well-being of individuals involved.

As society continues to evolve, it is imperative to recognize the need for legal reforms that acknowledge and protect the rights of individuals in live-in relationships. By providing legal recognition and safeguards, we can foster a more inclusive and equitable society that respects the choices and relationships of all individuals, irrespective of their marital status.

Introduction

Trust, commitment, and intimacy are foundational elements of any successful relationship, and they hold particular significance in the context of live-in relationships. In this chapter, we will delve into the importance of these three aspects and explore how couples can nurture and strengthen them within the framework of a non-traditional partnership.

Communication and Conflict Resolution

Open and effective communication forms the bedrock of trust, commitment, and intimacy. In live-in relationships, couples have the opportunity to engage in regular and ongoing conversations, which can deepen their understanding of each other and foster trust. It is essential to create a safe space where both partners feel comfortable expressing their thoughts, feelings, and concerns. Active listening, empathy, and validation are crucial tools that promote healthy communication.

Conflict is inevitable in any relationship, but it can be navigated in a constructive manner. In live-in relationships, conflicts can arise due to differences in living habits, financial matters, or personal boundaries. Couples should strive to resolve conflicts through dialogue rather than resorting to passive aggression or avoidance. Honesty, compromise, and a willingness to understand each other's perspectives can help to find mutually agreeable solutions and maintain trust within the relationship.

Individual Autonomy Versus Couple's Unity

Live-in relationships offer a unique dynamic where individuals can retain their autonomy while fostering a sense of unity as a couple. Balancing personal independence with shared goals and values requires trust and mutual respect. It is important to strike a healthy equilibrium where each partner feels supported in pursuing their individual aspirations while actively contributing to the growth and development of the relationship.

Respecting personal boundaries is a key aspect of individual autonomy. In a live-in relationship, partners may have different preferences regarding privacy, personal space, and time alone. Establishing clear boundaries and communicating them to each other helps maintain a sense of individuality and fosters trust and respect.

Financial Considerations in Live-in Relationships

Finances can be a sensitive topic in any relationship, and live-in partnerships are no exception. Discussing financial matters openly and honestly is essential to build trust and commitment. Couples should have conversations about income, expenses, and financial goals to ensure transparency and shared responsibility.

Decisions regarding joint expenses, savings, and financial planning should be made collaboratively, taking into account each partner's financial circumstances and aspirations. Some couples may choose to maintain separate bank accounts, while others may opt for joint accounts or a combination of both. The key is to find a financial arrangement that suits both partners and promotes trust and fairness.

Furthermore, couples should consider creating a contingency plan in the event of a separation or unforeseen circumstances. Addressing financial matters, such as asset division and financial support, through a prenuptial agreement or cohabitation agreement can provide clarity and peace of mind for both partners.

Intimacy

Intimacy goes beyond physical affection and encompasses emotional connection, vulnerability, and a deep understanding of each other. Nurturing intimacy requires ongoing effort and a willingness to prioritize emotional connection amidst the demands of daily life.

Quality time spent together is crucial for building and maintaining intimacy. Engaging in shared activities, expressing appreciation and affection, and actively listening to each other's thoughts and feelings can deepen the emotional bond. It is also important to foster an environment of emotional safety, where both partners feel comfortable expressing their true selves without fear of judgment or rejection.

In a live-in relationship, it is essential to strike a balance between togetherness and personal space. Allowing for individual interests and friendships outside the relationship can enrich the bond between partners, as it encourages personal growth and prevents feelings of suffocation or dependency.

Conclusion

Trust, commitment, and intimacy form the pillars of a successful and fulfilling live-in relationship. By nurturing open communication, addressing conflicts constructively, respecting individual autonomy, and fostering intimacy, couples can navigate the complexities of a non-traditional partnership. Financial considerations should also be discussed transparently and responsibly to ensure fairness and security. Ultimately, the strength of these elements will determine the long-term success and happiness of a live-in relationship.

Introduction

In modern society, the dynamics of relationships have evolved, and live-in partnerships have become increasingly common. Beyond the confines of traditional marriage, couples are choosing to share their lives and build a future together without the legal formalities. However, as with any committed relationship, financial matters and shared responsibilities play a significant role in fostering stability and harmony. In this chapter, we will explore the various aspects of sharing expenses and financial responsibilities in live-in relationships.

Property Rights and Ownership

One of the fundamental considerations in a live-in relationship is the issue of property rights and ownership. Unlike in marriage, where laws and regulations provide a clear framework for the division of assets in the event of separation or divorce, live-in partnerships operate in a legal gray area. In the absence of legal protection, it becomes crucial for couples to establish clear agreements regarding property ownership and the division of assets.

Couples should consider creating a cohabitation agreement, which outlines how property and assets will be owned and managed during the relationship and in the event of a breakup. This agreement can specify the contributions each partner makes towards property acquisition, mortgage payments, and other expenses. Additionally, it can address the allocation of assets accumulated during the relationship, such as investments, vehicles, and personal belongings.

Implications for Taxation and Insurance

Sharing expenses in a live-in relationship may have implications for taxation and insurance. Depending on the jurisdiction, tax laws may treat live-in partners differently from married couples or individuals living separately. It is essential to understand the tax regulations in your specific region and consult a professional to determine the most advantageous filing status and tax strategy for both partners.

Insurance coverage is another aspect to consider. In many cases, insurance policies, such as health, life, or car insurance, may not automatically extend to a live-in partner. Couples should review their insurance policies and ensure that their partners are adequately covered. This may require updating beneficiary designations, adding joint policies, or exploring alternative coverage options specifically designed for cohabiting couples.

Legal Aspects of Live-in Relationships

While live-in relationships offer greater flexibility and freedom than traditional marriages, it is crucial to understand the legal aspects and protections available to couples. Depending on the jurisdiction, common-law marriages or domestic partnerships may provide some legal recognition and benefits to live-in partners. Research the laws and regulations in your area to understand your rights and responsibilities as a live-in couple.

In the absence of legal recognition, it becomes even more important to establish clear agreements and documentation to protect both partners' interests. Cohabitation agreements, as mentioned earlier, can provide a framework for financial responsibilities, property ownership, and asset division. Additionally, partners may consider creating power of attorney documents, healthcare proxies, or wills to ensure that their wishes are respected and their partners have legal authority in case of incapacitation or death.

Conclusion

Live-in relationships offer a modern approach to partnership and commitment, but they also come with their own unique challenges. Sharing expenses and financial responsibilities is a crucial aspect of creating a stable and harmonious life together. By addressing issues related to property rights and ownership, understanding the implications for taxation and insurance, and exploring the legal aspects of live-in relationships, couples can navigate these challenges more effectively.

Open and honest communication, along with a willingness to create clear agreements and documentation, are key to ensuring financial stability and protecting the interests of both partners. Remember, every relationship is unique, and it is important to find solutions that work best for you and your partner. By proactively addressing financial matters, you can lay a solid foundation for a successful and fulfilling live-in partnership.

Introduction

In recent years, live-in relationships or cohabitation have gained significant popularity as an alternative to traditional marriage. As more individuals choose to live together without getting married, it becomes crucial to understand the laws and regulations that govern cohabitation. This chapter aims to explore the legal aspects surrounding cohabitation, including the rights and responsibilities of partners, the dissolution and separation processes, and the impact on parental and family relationships.

Rights and Responsibilities of Partners

While cohabiting couples may not have the same legal rights and protections as married couples, many jurisdictions have recognized certain legal rights and responsibilities for individuals in live-in relationships. These rights and responsibilities may vary depending on the jurisdiction, so it is essential for cohabiting partners to be aware of the laws specific to their location.

In some jurisdictions, cohabiting partners may have rights regarding property division, especially if they have jointly acquired assets or if one partner has contributed significantly to the other partner's property. However, it is crucial to note that property rights in cohabitation cases are often more complex and less protected than in marital cases.

Cohabiting partners may also have legal obligations towards each other, such as providing financial support or contributing to household expenses. These obligations can be determined through cohabitation agreements or recognized by the courts in cases where one partner has relied financially on the other.

Dissolution and Separation Processes

Just as marriages can come to an end, cohabitation relationships may also dissolve or separate. However, the processes and legal implications of ending a cohabitation relationship can differ significantly from those of divorce.

In the absence of legal frameworks specifically designed for cohabitation, the dissolution of a live-in relationship often involves resolving property disputes, determining custody and visitation arrangements for children (if applicable), and addressing financial obligations. The process can be more complex when couples have joint debts, shared property, or children.

To protect their interests, cohabiting partners can consider creating a cohabitation agreement, also known as a living together agreement or a domestic partnership agreement. This legally binding document can outline the division of assets, financial responsibilities, and child custody arrangements in the event of a separation.

It is worth noting that in some jurisdictions, common-law marriage or de facto relationships can grant certain legal rights and protections to cohabiting partners after a specific duration of cohabitation. However, these laws vary across jurisdictions, and it is crucial to consult local legislation or seek legal advice to understand the rights and obligations specific to a particular area.

Impact on Parental and Family Relationships

One of the significant aspects affected by cohabitation is parental and family relationships. When cohabiting couples have children together, it is important to consider the legal implications and rights associated with parenting.

In many jurisdictions, the biological mother of a child born within a cohabitation relationship automatically retains parental rights. However, the legal status of the non-biological parent may vary depending on the jurisdiction. Some jurisdictions recognize the non-biological parent as a legal parent if they have actively participated in the child's upbringing and have formed a significant parental bond.

In cases of separation or dissolution, the custody and visitation rights of cohabiting parents are typically determined based on the best interests of the child. Courts may consider factors such as the parent-child relationship, stability, and the ability to provide a suitable living environment when making custody and visitation decisions.

Conclusion

As cohabitation becomes more prevalent, it is crucial for individuals in live-in relationships to understand the laws and regulations concerning cohabitation in their jurisdiction. While cohabitation does not provide the same legal protections and rights as marriage, many jurisdictions have recognized certain rights and responsibilities for cohabiting partners. By being aware of their legal rights and obligations, individuals can make informed decisions and protect their interests in the event of separation or dissolution. Additionally, considering the impact on parental and family relationships is essential for cohabiting couples with children, as custody and visitation decisions can significantly affect the well-being of the children involved. Ultimately, navigating cohabitation requires a comprehensive understanding of the legal landscape to ensure the rights and responsibilities of all parties involved are respected and upheld.

Introduction

When it comes to live-in relationships, one significant challenge that couples often face is parental acceptance and objections. This chapter delves into the complexities surrounding parental attitudes towards live-in relationships and the impact it has on couples. We explore the effects on extended family dynamics, discuss strategies for handling parental disagreement and societal pressures, and touch upon the topic of live-in relationships and children.

Effects on Extended Family Dynamics

The decision to enter into a live-in relationship can disrupt the traditional dynamics within extended families. Parents and older generations often hold strong beliefs and values rooted in traditional norms, which can clash with the idea of unmarried couples cohabiting. This clash can lead to tensions, conflicts, and strained relationships within the family unit.

Parents may have concerns about the moral, social, and legal implications of their child living with a partner without being married. They may fear the judgment and scrutiny of society and worry about the impact on their own reputation. These concerns can create a rift between parents and their children, affecting the overall harmony of the family.

Handling Parental Disagreement and Societal Pressures

When faced with parental objections, it is crucial for couples in live-in relationships to navigate the situation with sensitivity and open communication. Here are some strategies that can help handle parental disagreement and societal pressures:

1. Respectful dialogue: Initiate an open and honest conversation with parents, expressing your thoughts and feelings regarding the live-in relationship. Listen attentively to their concerns and validate their perspectives, even if you disagree. By demonstrating respect and understanding, you can foster better communication and potentially ease their objections.

2. Education and awareness: Parents' objections often stem from a lack of understanding about live-in relationships. Provide them with information, research, and real-life examples that highlight the benefits and challenges of such arrangements. Encourage them to explore different perspectives and challenge preconceived notions.

3. Patience and empathy: It may take time for parents to come to terms with the idea of a live-in relationship. Be patient and empathetic towards their emotions, allowing them space to process their feelings. Assure them that your decision is not a rejection of their values but a choice that reflects your own beliefs and aspirations.

4. Seeking professional help: In some cases, involving a neutral third party, such as a family therapist or counselor, can be beneficial. A professional can facilitate constructive discussions, provide guidance, and help bridge the gap between differing viewpoints. Their expertise can help

family members navigate the complexities and find common ground.

Live-in Relationships and Children

One significant concern for parents is the impact of a live-in relationship on children, particularly if the couple decides to have children while cohabiting. Parents often worry about the stability, social acceptance, and legal rights of the child within such an arrangement.

Research suggests that children raised in stable and loving environments, whether within traditional marriages or live-in relationships, can thrive and develop positively. However, it is essential for couples to have open conversations about their expectations, parenting styles, and long-term plans before deciding to have children.

Legal considerations regarding custody, visitation rights, and financial responsibilities should also be thoroughly discussed and addressed. Seeking legal advice can help couples understand their rights and responsibilities, ensuring the best interests of the child are protected.

Conclusion

Parental acceptance and objections can significantly impact couples in live-in relationships. It is crucial for couples to approach these challenges with empathy, patience, and effective communication. By engaging in respectful dialogue, educating parents, and seeking professional help if needed, couples can foster understanding and acceptance within their families.

Moreover, addressing concerns about children in live-in relationships through open conversations and legal awareness can help create a supportive environment for the child's well-being. As society continues to evolve, it is essential for parents and couples to engage in compassionate dialogue and navigate the complexities of live-in relationships with empathy and understanding.

Introduction

In recent years, the traditional concept of marriage has undergone significant changes, with an increasing number of couples opting for live-in relationships as an alternative to formal marriage. With this shift, the dynamics of raising children have also evolved. This chapter explores the intricacies of raising children in a live-in relationship, highlighting the impact on child development and well-being, legal and social considerations for parenting in a non-marital context, and the socio-cultural perspectives surrounding live-in relationships.

Impact on Child Development and Well-being

One of the fundamental concerns when it comes to raising children in a live-in relationship is how it may affect their development and overall well-being. While research specifically focused on this topic is limited, studies on children raised in cohabiting households shed some light on the subject. It has been observed that the quality of the relationship between the parents and the level of stability within the relationship are crucial factors influencing a child's development.

Children raised in stable live-in relationships tend to fare well in terms of emotional and social development. Stability, open communication, and a healthy co-parenting dynamic are essential in providing a nurturing environment for children. When parents prioritize the well-being of their child and work together as a team, children can thrive irrespective of their parents' marital status.

However, it is important to acknowledge that conflicts and instability within a live-in relationship can have adverse effects on children. Frequent changes in parental partners or high levels of conflict can lead to emotional distress and uncertainty for children. Therefore, establishing a stable and supportive environment becomes even more crucial in live-in relationships to mitigate potential negative impacts on children.

Legal and Social Considerations for Parenting in a Non-Marital Context

Parenting within a live-in relationship often faces legal and social considerations that differ from those in a traditional marital context. In many jurisdictions, the legal rights and responsibilities of parents in a live-in relationship may not be as clearly defined as those in a marriage. This can lead to challenges related to custody, visitation rights, and financial support if the relationship were to dissolve.

To navigate these legal complexities, it is advisable for parents in a live-in relationship to consult legal professionals who specialize in family law. Establishing clear agreements and documentation regarding parental responsibilities, custody arrangements, and financial obligations can help protect the interests of both parents and the well-being of the child.

Society's perception of live-in relationships and parenting outside of marriage has also evolved over time. While societal attitudes vary across cultures and communities, there has been a gradual acceptance of non-traditional family structures. However, certain stigmas and biases may still exist, and parents in live-in relationships might encounter judgment or discrimination.

Open communication and education can play a crucial role in challenging societal prejudices. It is essential for parents to engage in conversations with family, friends, and their community to promote understanding and acceptance of their chosen family structure. Creating a supportive network of individuals who embrace diverse family configurations can help parents and children thrive in a live-in relationship.

Socio-cultural Perspectives on Live-in Relationships

Live-in relationships have been a part of various cultures throughout history, but their acceptance and prevalence have varied. Socio-cultural perspectives shape how live-in relationships and parenting outside of marriage are perceived and understood in different societies.

In some cultures, cohabitation may be deeply ingrained and widely accepted, with live-in relationships being viewed as equal to traditional marriages in terms of commitment and stability. These societies tend to focus more on the quality of the relationship and the well-being of the child rather than the legal or formal aspects of the arrangement.

On the other hand, certain cultures may still strongly adhere to traditional marital norms, considering live-in relationships as unconventional or morally objectionable. Such perspectives can pose challenges for parents in live-in relationships, as they may face societal pressures, discrimination, or even legal obstacles.

Conclusion

Raising children in a live-in relationship presents both opportunities and challenges. The impact on child development and well-being depends largely on the stability, communication, and co-parenting dynamics within the relationship. Legal and social considerations for parenting in a non-marital context require careful navigation and clear agreements to protect the interests of all parties involved.

Socio-cultural perspectives on live-in relationships vary across different communities, influencing societal acceptance and support. Promoting understanding and challenging biases through open communication can contribute to creating a more inclusive and accepting environment for families in live-in relationships.

Ultimately, the well-being and happiness of the child should be at the forefront of any parenting arrangement, whether within a traditional marriage or a live-in relationship. By prioritizing the needs of the child, fostering stability, and maintaining open lines of communication, parents can provide a nurturing environment that allows their children to thrive, regardless of their marital status.

Introduction

Cultural variations play a significant role in shaping societal attitudes and acceptance towards different relationship models. In the context of live-in relationships, understanding the influence of religion, traditions, and changing societal norms is crucial. This chapter delves into these aspects, exploring how cultural variations impact the acceptance of live-in relationships. Additionally, it examines the dynamics between live-in relationships and marriage, questioning whether they represent a transition or a choice for separation.

Influence of Religion and Traditions

Religion often plays a central role in determining the cultural values and beliefs of a community. Different religious doctrines and practices can significantly shape societal attitudes towards relationships. In some cultures, religious teachings may emphasize the importance of traditional marriage as the only acceptable form of union. This can create challenges for the acceptance of live-in relationships, as they may be viewed as a departure from the prescribed norms.

However, it is important to recognize that religious perspectives on relationships are not uniform across all faiths and denominations. Some religions are more open to alternative relationship models, while others may be more conservative. For example, in certain Hindu sects, the practice of "Gandharva Vivaha" acknowledges the legitimacy of live-in relationships, highlighting the diverse interpretations within religions themselves.

Moreover, traditions rooted in cultural practices can also influence societal acceptance. In some cultures, arranged marriages are deeply ingrained, and the idea of choosing one's partner outside the bounds of marriage can be met with resistance. These traditional practices can create barriers to accepting live-in relationships, as they challenge the existing social order.

Changing Societal Norms and Attitudes

Societal norms and attitudes towards relationships are not static; they evolve over time. As societies become more diverse and globalized, the acceptance of different relationship models, including live-in relationships, is gradually increasing. Urbanization, exposure to different cultures, and the rise of individualism have all contributed to shifting societal attitudes.

In many Western societies, live-in relationships have gained wider acceptance over the past few decades. The focus has shifted from the institution of marriage as the sole framework for committed partnerships to recognizing the importance of personal choice and individual happiness. However, it is essential to acknowledge that acceptance levels may still vary within different regions, subcultures, and generations.

In contrast, some societies still struggle with deeply ingrained traditional beliefs, where the notion of living together without marriage remains highly stigmatized. These societies may face challenges in accepting live-in relationships due to the fear of undermining family structures or deviating from established cultural norms.

Live-in Relationships and Marriage: Transitioning or Choosing Separation

The relationship between live-in partnerships and marriage is a complex one. While some view live-in relationships as a stepping stone towards marriage, others perceive them as a deliberate choice to deviate from traditional norms. In some cases, live-in relationships can provide an opportunity for couples to test compatibility and explore their long-term compatibility before committing to marriage.

However, it is important to note that not all couples in live-in relationships aspire to marry. For some individuals, marriage may not align with their personal values, goals, or life choices. Live-in relationships can offer an alternative to marriage, allowing couples to maintain their autonomy while building a committed partnership.

The transitioning from a live-in relationship to marriage or choosing separation is highly individual and influenced by personal beliefs, values, and circumstances. It is crucial to respect each person's agency in deciding what relationship model best suits their needs and aspirations.

Conclusion

Cultural variations significantly impact the acceptance of live-in relationships. The influence of religion, traditions, and changing societal norms shape attitudes towards these alternative relationship models. While some cultures embrace live-in relationships as a valid choice, others may view them as a departure from established norms.

As societies evolve, attitudes towards live-in relationships are gradually shifting. Increasing exposure to diverse cultures, urbanization, and changing perspectives on individual happiness contribute to greater acceptance in some regions. However, cultural and religious beliefs deeply rooted in tradition can present barriers to acceptance in certain societies.

Understanding the dynamics between live-in relationships and marriage is essential. While some view live-in partnerships as a precursor to marriage, others consciously choose separation from the institution of marriage. Each individual's personal beliefs and circumstances influence their choices, and it is important to respect and validate diverse relationship models.

By acknowledging and exploring the cultural variations and acceptance of live-in relationships, we can foster a more inclusive and understanding society that respects the autonomy and choices of individuals in their pursuit of fulfilling relationships.

Introduction

Live-in relationships have become increasingly prevalent in modern society, providing couples with an alternative path to traditional marriage. These relationships offer a unique dynamic that requires thoughtful navigation and decision-making. In this chapter, we will explore the various milestones that couples in live-in relationships may encounter and the importance of effective decision-making throughout the journey.

Transitioning from Live-in to Marriage

One significant milestone that may arise in a live-in relationship is the decision to transition to marriage. This transition is a deeply personal and individual choice that requires open and honest communication between partners. When contemplating marriage, it is essential to reflect on the reasons behind this decision. Is it driven by societal expectations, personal values, or a genuine desire to commit to a lifelong partnership?

During this phase, couples should engage in heartfelt conversations to align their expectations, goals, and values. Discussing important topics such as finances, family planning, career aspirations, and long-term visions will help ensure compatibility and shared understanding. It is crucial to recognize that the decision to marry should stem from a place of mutual love, respect, and commitment rather than external pressures or expectations.

Considerations for Ending a Live-in Relationship

While every couple hopes for a successful and fulfilling live-in relationship, it is important to acknowledge that not all unions will stand the test of time. Ending a live-in relationship is a significant decision that can bring about a wide range of emotions. When contemplating a separation, it is crucial to consider the following factors.

1. Reflection and introspection: Before making the decision to end a live-in relationship, both partners should take time for self-reflection. Assessing personal needs, desires, and levels of satisfaction within the relationship can shed light on whether it is salvageable or if it is time to part ways.

2. Communication: Open and honest communication is paramount when considering the end of a live-in relationship. Both partners should express their feelings, concerns, and desires with empathy and respect. Constructive dialogue can help identify areas of growth, potential solutions, or the realization that separation is the best path forward.

3. Seeking professional help: If the relationship is experiencing significant challenges, seeking the guidance of a couples therapist or counselor can provide valuable insights and facilitate effective decision-making. A neutral third party can help navigate complex emotions and offer strategies for potential reconciliation or an amicable separation.

Communication and Conflict Resolution in Live-in Relationships

Effective communication and conflict resolution skills are vital in any relationship, and live-in partnerships are no exception. To build a strong foundation for a successful live-in relationship, couples should prioritize open and honest communication while addressing conflicts constructively.

1. Active listening: Active listening involves giving full attention to one's partner without interrupting or formulating responses prematurely. This practice promotes understanding and empathy, allowing partners to connect on a deeper level.

2. Expressing emotions: Sharing emotions honestly and respectfully is crucial for fostering emotional intimacy. By expressing feelings openly, couples can avoid misunderstandings and work together to find mutually satisfying solutions.

3. Managing conflict: Conflict is inevitable in any relationship, but how couples navigate it determines the health and longevity of the partnership. Conflict resolution techniques such as compromising, finding win-win solutions, and practicing forgiveness can help address differences and maintain a harmonious coexistence.

Conclusion

Live-in relationships offer a path beyond traditional marriage, enabling couples to explore commitment and partnership on their own terms. Throughout this journey, couples encounter various milestones that require careful consideration and decision-making. Whether it involves transitioning to marriage or contemplating the end of a live-in relationship, open communication, empathy, and self-reflection are essential.

By fostering effective communication and conflict resolution skills, couples can nurture the bonds of their live-in relationships. The ability to express emotions, actively listen, and manage conflicts constructively promotes growth, understanding, and mutual satisfaction.

Ultimately, the success of a live-in relationship lies in the hands of the individuals involved. By embracing the milestones and decisions that arise, couples can navigate their live-in relationships with grace, intention, and a shared commitment to personal and relational growth.

Introduction

Communication is the foundation of any successful relationship, and this holds true for live-in relationships as well. In a society where traditional marriage is not the only path to commitment and companionship, it becomes essential to explore effective communication strategies to nurture and navigate the complexities of live-in relationships. This chapter will delve into the various aspects of communication that are vital for building a strong and sustainable partnership beyond traditional marriage.

Handling Conflicts and Disagreements

Conflicts and disagreements are inevitable in any relationship, including live-in arrangements. However, the key to maintaining harmony lies in how these conflicts are managed. Effective communication during such times can help in resolving issues and strengthening the bond between partners.

First and foremost, it is essential to approach conflicts with an open mind and willingness to listen. Active listening plays a crucial role in effective communication. Each partner should have the opportunity to express their thoughts and feelings without judgment or interruption. This creates a safe space for open dialogue and enables both parties to understand each other's perspectives.

When conflicts arise, it is important to focus on the problem at hand rather than attacking the person. Using "I" statements instead of "you" statements can prevent blame and defensiveness from escalating the situation. For instance, saying, "I feel hurt when this happens" is more constructive than saying, "You always make me feel hurt."

It is also crucial to choose the right time and place to address conflicts. Timing matters, and discussing sensitive issues when both partners are calm and receptive can lead to more productive conversations. Moreover, creating a comfortable environment free from distractions can foster effective communication and facilitate problem-solving.

Nurturing a Healthy and Balanced Relationship

Beyond traditional marriage, live-in relationships require intentional effort to create and maintain a healthy and balanced partnership. Effective communication serves as the backbone of this endeavor. Here are a few strategies to nurture such a relationship:

1. Expressing Appreciation: Regularly expressing appreciation for each other's efforts and qualities can strengthen the emotional connection. Simple gestures like saying "thank you" and acknowledging each other's contributions can go a long way in fostering positivity and reinforcing mutual respect.

2. Setting Boundaries: Establishing clear boundaries is vital in any relationship, including live-in arrangements. Effective communication helps partners discuss and define personal boundaries, thereby ensuring mutual understanding and respect for each other's space, privacy, and individuality.

3. Regular Check-ins: Consistent communication is essential to keep the relationship healthy and thriving. Regular check-ins, where partners discuss their feelings, aspirations, and any concerns, can help prevent misunderstandings and maintain emotional intimacy.

4. Empathy and Understanding: Cultivating empathy and understanding is crucial in a live-in relationship. Effective communication involves actively listening and trying to comprehend each other's emotions and experiences. This empathetic approach creates a supportive and compassionate environment, promoting emotional well-being.

Sexual Intimacy in Live-in Relationships

Sexual intimacy is an integral part of many live-in relationships. However, discussing and navigating this aspect requires open and honest communication between partners. Here are some key points to consider:

1. Establishing Consent: Consent is of utmost importance in any sexual relationship. Partners should communicate their desires, boundaries, and limits clearly and obtain mutual consent before engaging in any sexual activities. Consent should be ongoing and never assumed.

2. Creating a Safe Environment: Effective communication plays a significant role in creating a safe and comfortable environment for discussing sexual desires, concerns, and fantasies. It allows partners to openly express their needs, enabling them to explore and enhance their sexual intimacy together.

3. Discussing Expectations: Each partner may have different expectations regarding sexual frequency,

preferences, and experimentation. Open dialogue helps partners understand each other's desires, avoid assumptions, and find a mutually satisfying balance.

4. Seeking Professional Help: In some cases, couples may encounter challenges related to sexual intimacy that require professional guidance. Effective communication helps partners discuss these concerns and seek the assistance of a sex therapist or counselor who specializes in relationships.

Conclusion

Effective communication is a vital component of successful live-in relationships. It enables partners to handle conflicts and disagreements constructively, nurtures a healthy and balanced relationship, and facilitates open dialogue about sexual intimacy. By actively practicing and prioritizing effective communication strategies, couples can build strong foundations, foster emotional intimacy, and navigate the complexities of live-in relationships with trust and understanding. Remember, communication is the key to unlocking a fulfilling and thriving partnership beyond traditional marriage.

Introduction

Sexual compatibility is a crucial aspect of any romantic relationship, including live-in relationships. While love, trust, and shared values form the foundation of a strong partnership, a fulfilling and satisfying sexual connection is equally important for long-term relationship success. In this chapter, we will explore the significance of sexual compatibility in live-in relationships and how it contributes to overall relationship satisfaction and well-being.

Maintaining Intimacy and Desire

One of the primary reasons sexual compatibility is vital in a live-in relationship is its role in maintaining intimacy and desire between partners. As the initial excitement of a new relationship settles into a more comfortable routine, it is essential to cultivate a vibrant sexual connection to keep the flame alive. A strong sexual bond enhances emotional closeness, fosters deeper intimacy, and contributes to overall relationship satisfaction.

Addressing Challenges and Seeking Help

In live-in relationships, it is not uncommon for couples to encounter challenges in their sexual relationship. These challenges can range from differences in sexual desires and preferences to difficulties in communication or physical issues. The key to overcoming these challenges lies in open and honest communication. By discussing desires, boundaries, and concerns, couples can work together to find solutions that satisfy both partners. It is important to create a safe space where individuals feel comfortable expressing their needs and seeking compromises.

In some cases, professional help may be beneficial. Sex therapists and relationship counselors are trained to address sexual issues and provide guidance on improving sexual compatibility. Seeking outside help does not indicate failure but rather a proactive approach to enhancing the relationship's overall well-being. Remember, every relationship is unique, and seeking assistance is a positive step towards growth and improvement.

Cohabitation Agreements and Legal Protection

While sexual compatibility is primarily about emotional and physical fulfillment, it is also prudent to address practical matters within a live-in relationship. Cohabitation agreements can play a vital role in protecting both partners' rights and ensuring a fair and equitable resolution in case of a breakup or separation. These agreements outline responsibilities, property rights, financial arrangements, and other considerations specific to the relationship.

When it comes to sexual compatibility, it is important to note that a lack thereof does not automatically warrant a breakup or dissolution of the relationship. Sometimes, couples may face challenges in this area, but through open communication, willingness to explore, and seeking professional help, they can work towards finding common ground. However, if efforts to improve sexual compatibility prove unsuccessful, it is crucial to evaluate the overall satisfaction and happiness within the relationship.

Conclusion

Sexual compatibility holds immense importance in live-in relationships. It contributes to maintaining intimacy, desire, and overall relationship satisfaction. Open and honest communication, along with a willingness to address challenges and seek help when needed, is crucial for nurturing a healthy sexual connection. Additionally, practical considerations such as cohabitation agreements can provide legal protection and ensure fair resolutions. Remember, every relationship is unique, and sexual compatibility is just one piece of the puzzle. By prioritizing communication, understanding, and respect, couples can navigate the intricacies of live-in relationships and build a strong foundation for a fulfilling and harmonious life together.

Introduction

In recent years, there has been a significant shift in societal norms surrounding relationships, leading to an increase in the number of couples choosing to live together without getting married. Cohabitation, or living together outside of marriage, has become a popular choice for many individuals seeking companionship and shared responsibilities without the legal and social commitments associated with marriage. However, it's crucial to recognize that cohabitation also involves financial, property, and legal considerations that need to be addressed to protect the interests and rights of both partners involved. This chapter explores the importance of understanding cohabitation agreements in navigating live-in relationships.

Financial and Property Matters

One of the primary aspects to consider in a cohabitation agreement is the financial and property matters. Unlike marriage, cohabitation does not automatically grant legal rights to each partner's assets, incomes, or debts. Therefore, it becomes crucial for couples to outline their financial expectations and responsibilities through a cohabitation agreement.

A cohabitation agreement can include provisions for how expenses will be shared, such as rent or mortgage payments, utility bills, and household expenses. It can also establish guidelines for handling joint bank accounts or other financial assets accumulated during the relationship.

Additionally, property ownership is another vital consideration. Without a cohabitation agreement, disputes may arise regarding the ownership of property, especially if only one partner's name is on the title. A well-drafted cohabitation agreement can clarify property rights and ensure that each partner's contributions to the property are recognized and protected.

Safeguarding Interests and Rights

Cohabitation agreements serve as a means to safeguard the interests and rights of both partners involved. These agreements can address various aspects, including property rights, inheritance, and even the division of assets in the event of separation or death.

For example, a cohabitation agreement can specify what happens to the property if the relationship ends. It can outline how assets will be divided and provide a clear process for resolving any disputes that may arise. By addressing these matters beforehand, couples can minimize potential conflicts and ensure a fair and equitable distribution of assets.

In the unfortunate event of death, a cohabitation agreement can also protect the surviving partner's interests. Without such an agreement, the surviving partner may face legal challenges in terms of inheritance and property rights. A well-crafted cohabitation agreement can establish the rights and obligations of each partner, ensuring that their wishes are respected and legally enforceable.

Impact on Mental Health and Well-being

Understanding and having a cohabitation agreement can have a significant impact on the mental health and well-being of individuals in live-in relationships. When couples establish clear expectations and guidelines through a cohabitation agreement, it reduces uncertainty and provides a sense of security within the relationship.

Cohabitation agreements can help alleviate stress and anxiety that may arise from financial uncertainties, property disputes, or concerns about future contingencies. By addressing these matters upfront, couples can focus on building a healthy and fulfilling relationship, knowing that their interests and rights are protected.

Furthermore, discussing and drafting a cohabitation agreement requires open communication and mutual understanding between partners. This process allows couples to engage in important conversations about their values, goals, and expectations, strengthening their bond and promoting a healthier relationship dynamic.

Conclusion

Living together outside of marriage has become a common choice for many couples, but it is essential to recognize the importance of understanding cohabitation agreements. These agreements play a vital role in clarifying financial and property matters, safeguarding interests and rights, and promoting the mental health and well-being of individuals in live-in relationships.

By addressing financial responsibilities, property ownership, and potential future contingencies through a cohabitation agreement, couples can navigate the complexities of cohabitation with confidence. These agreements provide a legal framework that ensures fairness, protects individual interests, and fosters open communication between partners.

In a world where traditional marriage is no longer the only path to commitment, cohabitation agreements offer a practical and effective means for couples to establish their rights, protect their assets, and build strong and lasting relationships. By understanding and embracing the importance of cohabitation agreements, couples can navigate the uncharted territory of live-in relationships with clarity and peace of mind.

Chapter 15. Psychological implications of live-in relationships

Introduction

Live-in relationships have become increasingly common in modern society, challenging the traditional notions of marriage and commitment. These relationships, characterized by cohabitation without legal marriage, come with their own set of psychological implications. In this chapter, we will explore the psychological aspects of live-in relationships, focusing on managing stress and emotional challenges, seeking professional support when needed, and the importance of social support and networking.

Managing Stress and Emotional Challenges

Live-in relationships, like any other form of intimate partnership, can bring about various stressors and emotional challenges. Sharing a living space and daily routines with a partner can lead to conflicts, differences in expectations, and compromises. It is crucial for individuals in live-in relationships to develop effective strategies for managing these stressors and maintaining emotional well-being.

1. Communication: Open and honest communication is the foundation of any healthy relationship. In a live-in arrangement, effective communication becomes even more important. Expressing one's needs, concerns, and emotions in a respectful manner can help address conflicts and prevent resentment from building up.

2. Boundaries and Privacy: Living together can blur the lines between personal and shared space. It is essential for individuals in live-in relationships to establish boundaries and respect each other's need for privacy. Maintaining individual interests, hobbies, and social circles can contribute to personal fulfillment and reduce dependency on the relationship.

3. Conflict Resolution: Conflicts are a natural part of any relationship. Learning constructive conflict resolution skills, such as active listening, compromise, and empathy, can enhance the quality of a live-in relationship. Recognizing the importance of finding win-win solutions and avoiding destructive patterns, like blame or defensiveness, can help maintain a healthy emotional environment.

Seeking Professional Support if Needed

While most live-in relationships are successful, some individuals may encounter significant emotional or psychological challenges that require professional support. It is crucial to recognize when seeking help from a therapist or counselor could be beneficial. Here are some scenarios where professional assistance may be warranted:

1. Unresolved Emotional Baggage: Individuals entering a live-in relationship may carry emotional baggage from past experiences, such as previous relationships or childhood trauma. These unresolved issues can negatively impact the dynamics of the current relationship. Seeking therapy can provide a safe space to process and heal from these emotional wounds, leading to healthier relationship patterns.

2. Intimacy and Sexual Concerns: Sexual intimacy plays a significant role in most romantic relationships. However, issues such as differences in desire, performance anxiety, or unresolved sexual trauma can arise. Consulting a sex therapist or relationship counselor can help address these concerns, fostering a more fulfilling intimate connection.

3. Relationship Transitions: Live-in relationships can undergo transitions, such as considering marriage, starting a family, or even ending the cohabitation. These changes can bring about a range of emotions and uncertainties. Seeking professional guidance during these pivotal moments can provide clarity, support decision-making, and facilitate effective communication between partners.

Social Support and Networking in Live-in Relationships

Live-in relationships can benefit from a robust support system beyond the couple themselves. Building and maintaining a network of supportive friends and family members can contribute to the overall well-being of individuals in live-in relationships. Here are some reasons why social support is important:

1. Emotional Validation: Having a support network allows individuals to share their experiences, emotions, and concerns with trusted confidants. Feeling heard and understood by others can validate one's feelings and provide a sense of reassurance and belonging.

2. Perspective and Advice: Friends and family members can offer valuable perspectives and advice based on their own experiences. Different viewpoints can shed light on challenges and help navigate complex situations in live-in relationships.

3. Recreational and Social Activities: Participating in social activities together as a couple or within a larger social circle can enhance the overall quality of the relationship. Engaging in shared hobbies, outings, or celebrations can create positive memories and strengthen the bond between partners.

Conclusion

Live-in relationships offer a unique approach to intimacy and commitment, challenging the traditional boundaries of marriage. Understanding and addressing the psychological implications of such relationships is essential for maintaining their long-term success. By managing stress and emotional challenges, seeking professional support when needed, and fostering social support and networking, individuals in live-in relationships can navigate the complexities and enjoy the many benefits that these relationships have to offer.

Introduction

In the realm of relationships, the concept of marriage has long held a central position. However, societal norms are evolving, and people are increasingly exploring alternative relationship models that go beyond traditional marriage. One such model gaining popularity is the idea of live-in relationships, where couples choose to live together without getting married. This chapter delves into the importance of building a support system outside of marriage in the context of live-in relationships. By leveraging community resources and networks, addressing isolation and loneliness, and recognizing cultural shifts and future trends, individuals in live-in relationships can create a robust and fulfilling support system that enhances their well-being.

Community Resources and Networks

In the absence of the legal and social support traditionally provided by marriage, it becomes crucial for individuals in live-in relationships to tap into community resources and networks. These resources can range from local community centers and support groups to online forums and social media communities. Such platforms offer opportunities to connect with like-minded individuals who share similar relationship dynamics and challenges. By actively participating in these networks, individuals can find valuable advice, emotional support, and practical solutions to navigate the intricacies of their live-in relationships.

Additionally, community resources often provide access to professional counseling services, workshops, and educational programs tailored specifically for couples in non-marital relationships. These avenues can offer valuable guidance on communication, conflict resolution, and relationship dynamics, enabling couples to strengthen their bond and build a solid foundation for their live-in arrangement.

Addressing Isolation and Loneliness

One of the potential pitfalls of live-in relationships is the increased risk of isolation and loneliness. Without the formal recognition and support of marriage, individuals may find themselves lacking the same level of social validation and connection that married couples often enjoy. However, it is important to recognize that live-in relationships can offer unique opportunities for personal growth and self-discovery.

To combat feelings of isolation, individuals in live-in relationships should proactively seek out social activities and cultivate friendships outside of their partnership. Engaging in hobbies, joining clubs or interest groups, and attending social events can help expand one's social circle and create a sense of belonging. These activities not only alleviate feelings of loneliness but also contribute to personal fulfillment and overall happiness.

Moreover, it is crucial for individuals in live-in relationships to maintain strong connections with their existing support systems, such as family and friends. By nurturing these relationships, individuals can ensure they have a reliable network of emotional support, guidance, and practical assistance, which is invaluable for navigating the complexities of a non-marital partnership.

Cultural Shifts and Future Trends

The rise in popularity of live-in relationships signifies a broader cultural shift towards a more inclusive understanding of intimate partnerships. As societal norms continue to evolve, it is essential to anticipate and adapt to future trends that may impact the support systems available to individuals in non-marital relationships.

Legal frameworks surrounding cohabitation and partnership rights are gradually adapting to accommodate the changing relationship landscape. It is important for individuals in live-in relationships to stay informed about legal developments and seek legal advice when necessary. This ensures they are aware of their rights, responsibilities, and available legal protections, which can significantly impact their support system.

Furthermore, as live-in relationships become more widely accepted, it is anticipated that community resources and networks tailored specifically for non-marital partnerships will continue to emerge. This expansion will create even more opportunities for individuals in live-in relationships to connect, share experiences, and access specialized support services that cater to their unique needs.

Conclusion

Building a support system outside of marriage is a vital aspect of navigating live-in relationships successfully. By leveraging community resources and networks, individuals can tap into valuable advice, guidance, and emotional support. Additionally, addressing isolation and loneliness is crucial, and individuals should actively cultivate friendships, engage in social activities, and maintain connections with existing support systems. Looking ahead, it is important to stay informed about cultural shifts and future trends that may impact the support available for non-marital relationships. By actively participating in these evolving dynamics, individuals in live-in relationships can create a robust and fulfilling support system that enriches their lives and strengthens their bonds.

Chapter 17. Emerging patterns in live-in relationships

Introduction

Live-in relationships have become increasingly common in recent years, challenging the traditional notions of marriage and commitment. As societal attitudes continue to evolve, more individuals are choosing to explore alternative forms of partnership that prioritize personal freedom, flexibility, and shared responsibilities. This chapter delves into the emerging patterns in live-in relationships, examining the shifting attitudes towards marriage and commitment, projecting future societal changes, and offering insights on how to navigate these relationships successfully.

Attitudes towards Marriage and Commitment

One of the key factors driving the rise of live-in relationships is the changing attitudes towards marriage and commitment. In the past, marriage was often seen as the only socially acceptable form of long-term partnership, providing legal and societal recognition. However, modern society has witnessed a significant shift in these perspectives.

Many individuals today value personal freedom and autonomy, and traditional marriage may be viewed as restrictive or outdated. Live-in relationships offer a middle ground where couples can enjoy the benefits of companionship, emotional support, and shared responsibilities without the formalities and legal entanglements associated with marriage. This shift in attitudes has led to a growing acceptance of live-in relationships as a valid and fulfilling choice for couples.

Moreover, the decline in religious influence and the rise of individualism have played a role in reshaping societal perceptions of commitment. Couples no longer feel compelled to conform to traditional norms and instead seek relationships that align with their personal values and desires. Live-in relationships provide the flexibility to adapt to changing circumstances and allow individuals to redefine commitment on their own terms.

Projecting Future Societal Changes

The emerging patterns in live-in relationships are likely to have a profound impact on society in the coming years. Here are some projected societal changes that could arise from this shift:

1. Legal recognition: As live-in relationships become more prevalent, legal frameworks may adapt to provide rights and protections for couples in these arrangements. This could involve creating specific laws or contractual agreements to address issues such as property rights, inheritance, and child custody.

2. Changing family dynamics: Live-in relationships challenge the traditional family structure, prompting a redefinition of family dynamics. Blended families, where individuals with children from previous relationships cohabit, may become more common. This will require a shift in societal attitudes towards non-traditional family units and the provision of adequate support systems.

3. Economic implications: Live-in relationships often involve shared financial responsibilities. This can have

economic implications, such as joint property ownership, shared expenses, and tax considerations. Financial institutions and policymakers may need to adapt to cater to the unique needs and challenges faced by couples in live-in relationships.

4. Social acceptance: Over time, live-in relationships are likely to become more widely accepted and normalized. As more individuals choose this form of partnership, societal stigmas surrounding live-in relationships may diminish. However, cultural and generational differences may influence the pace of acceptance in different regions.

Navigating Live-in Relationships Successfully

For individuals considering or already engaged in live-in relationships, navigating the complexities of these partnerships can be both exciting and challenging. Here are some insights to help couples navigate live-in relationships successfully:

1. Open communication: Clear and open communication is essential for any relationship, but it becomes even more crucial in a live-in arrangement. Discuss expectations, boundaries, and long-term goals to ensure both partners are on the same page.

2. Shared responsibilities: Live-in relationships often involve sharing financial responsibilities, household chores, and decision-making. Establish a fair division of responsibilities based on each partner's strengths, preferences, and availability. Regularly revisit and adjust these arrangements as needed.

3. Building trust: Trust is the foundation of any successful relationship. In a live-in partnership, trust becomes even

more important as couples navigate shared living spaces and personal boundaries. Foster trust through honesty, respect, and consistent support for each other.

4. Flexibility and adaptability: Live-in relationships offer flexibility, but they also require adaptability. As circumstances change, be open to adjusting living arrangements, financial arrangements, and expectations. Embrace the fluid nature of these relationships and approach challenges as opportunities for growth.

Conclusion

The emergence of live-in relationships as a viable alternative to traditional marriage reflects the evolving attitudes and values of modern society. As individuals seek greater autonomy, personal freedom, and flexibility in their partnerships, live-in relationships offer a compelling option. With open communication, shared responsibilities, trust, and adaptability, couples can navigate these relationships successfully. As society continues to evolve, it is essential to recognize and respect the diverse forms of commitment that individuals choose, allowing for greater inclusivity and understanding in our ever-changing world.

Introduction

Embarking on a live-in relationship marks a significant departure from traditional notions of marriage. It is a journey filled with excitement, uncertainty, and personal growth. As we navigate the complexities of this modern dynamic, it becomes essential to reflect on our experiences and gain insights into the unique challenges and rewards that accompany live-in relationships. In this chapter, we will delve into the profound reflections on the journey of living together outside the confines of traditional marriage.

Balancing Individual Needs and Relationship Dynamics

One of the fundamental aspects of a successful live-in relationship is the delicate balance between individual needs and the dynamics of the partnership. In a society where individualism is increasingly emphasized, it is crucial to recognize and respect the desires, aspirations, and personal space of both partners. Living together allows for a deeper understanding of each other's individual needs, and it is essential to create an environment that fosters personal growth and fulfillment.

Reflection prompts us to contemplate how we can strike a harmonious balance between autonomy and togetherness. It requires open and honest communication, active listening, and a willingness to compromise. Each partner must be willing to acknowledge their own desires while considering the needs of their significant other. It is through this delicate dance of understanding and compromise that we can create a strong foundation for our live-in relationship to thrive.

Making Informed Decisions about the Future

Living together in a committed relationship inevitably raises questions about the future. While traditional marriages often come with established societal expectations and legal frameworks, live-in relationships offer greater flexibility and fluidity. This freedom can be both liberating and challenging, as it requires us to proactively engage in making informed decisions about our shared future.

Reflection allows us to explore and discuss important aspects such as financial planning, long-term goals, and potential commitment levels. It is an opportunity to ask ourselves and our partners difficult questions: What are our shared aspirations? How do we envision our future together? What legal and financial protections do we need to consider? By engaging in these reflections, we empower ourselves to make conscious choices and take proactive steps towards shaping a future that aligns with our values and desires.

In our reflections, we might encounter societal expectations or pressures that can influence our decision-making process. It is important to critically examine these external factors and discern what truly resonates with us and our relationship. Each couple's journey is unique, and our decisions should be guided by our own understanding and needs rather than external judgments or traditional norms.

Conclusion

The journey of a live-in relationship is a transformative one that challenges traditional paradigms and encourages personal growth. Reflections along the way provide us with invaluable insights into the delicate balance between individual needs and relationship dynamics. They guide us in making informed decisions about our future, allowing us to shape a path that aligns with our values and aspirations.

As we continue to navigate the uncharted territories of live-in relationships, it is essential to embrace open and honest communication, active listening, and a commitment to personal growth. By engaging in regular reflections, we deepen our understanding of ourselves and our partners, fostering a sense of emotional intimacy and connection.

Beyond the constraints of traditional marriage, live-in relationships offer an opportunity for personal fulfillment and the creation of unique and authentic partnerships. Through reflection, we can navigate the challenges and celebrate the rewards of this journey, ultimately forging a path that transcends societal norms and leads to a more meaningful and fulfilling life together.

"Beyond Traditional Marriage: Navigating Live-in Relationships" explores the concept of live-in relationships, distinguishing them from dating and marriage. It discusses the benefits of flexibility and freedom, as well as the challenges of lacking legal protection. The book covers trust, commitment, intimacy, sharing expenses, and financial responsibilities. It also addresses cohabitation laws, parental acceptance, raising children, cultural variations, communication strategies, sexual compatibility, cohabitation agreements, psychological implications, building support systems, and emerging relationship patterns. Reflective insights are provided on the journey of couples in non-traditional partnerships.

ABOUT THE AUTHOR

Mr. C. P. Kumar is a retired Scientist 'G' from National Institute of Hydrology, Roorkee, Uttarakhand, India. He is also a Reiki Healer and Chakra Balancing practitioner (with pendulum dowsing) and offers Emotional Freedom Technique (EFT) to help individuals with emotional issues. Mr. Kumar has authored many books on technical, spiritual, and social topics.

For further details, you may visit his webpage
https://www.angelfire.com/nh/cpkumar/virgo.html

www.ingramcontent.com/pod-product-compliance
Lightning Source LLC
Chambersburg PA
CBHW050603160726
48003CB00003B/1030

9798223127802